THE KEY
TO THE TAROT

THE KEY
TO THE TAROT

JANE LYLE

HarperSanFrancisco
A Division of HarperCollins*Publishers*

Frontispiece:
The Magician. Italian design by Bonifacio Bembo, fifteenth century.

FIRST HARPERCOLLINS EDITION PUBLISHED IN 1995

Printed in Singapore.

ISBN 0-06-251133-5

94 95 96 97 98 SGP 10 9 8 7 6 5 4 3 2 1

INTRODUCTION

The Tarot deck we know today contains seventy-eight cards. Of these, twenty-two are known as the Major Arcana, or Greater Secrets – cards depicting strange, dream-like images such as The Angel of Temperance and The Tower Struck by Lightning. The remaining fifty-six cards form what is known as the Minor Arcana, or Lesser Secrets. These cards are the parents of our familiar playing cards, minus the four knights of Tarot – while the only Major Arcana figure to have survived in these decks is The Fool, now known as The Joker.

It is the fifth suit, or Major Arcana, which evokes the most fascination – for its origins are swathed in mystery while its images are both alluring and disturbing. Where did it come from? China, Ancient Egypt, and India are variously supposed to have been the birthplace of Tarot.

Tarot's Legendary Origins

One legend has it that there was once a great library, containing all the wisdom of the ancients, at Alexandria in Egypt. When the libary was destroyed, the city of Fez became the focal point for mystics, philosophers and wise men from all over the world who devised a special pictorial language to communicate with one another. These images spoke of universal spiritual truths and esoteric teachings, still linked with Tarot today.

Gypsies are said to have brought the cards to Europe from their original home in India. Since the word 'gypsy' is thought to be a corruption of the word 'Egyptian', this theory links two of the sources rather neatly.

While we can but speculate on the origins of Tarot, we do know that its images are inextricably linked to ancient beliefs and mythologies. There are obvious correspondences with the Hebrew cabala, numerology, Gnosticism and Celtic religion.

The Devil's Picture Book

Early versions of the cards themselves surfaced in Europe during the fourteenth century. They were brought by Crusaders returning from the land of the Saracens, and were rapidly condemned by the established Church as heretical. During the years which followed they were banned and burned in Germany, France and Italy. But they survived. The earliest Tarot cards still in existence date from 1392; seventeen of them are left. The first entire deck to have survived is dated thirty years later, painted by the Italian Bonifacio Bembo for the Duke of Milan.

Tarot cards were always referred to as a 'book' – whether the gypsies' 'bible' or the churchman's 'devil's picture book'. Many scholars believe that they were a way of preserving 'heretical' knowledge at a time when it was dangerous to believe in anything other than established dogma.

But whatever their history, the cards do indeed tell a story. It is the story of an adventure, filled with challenges, obstacles to be overcome, and lessons to be absorbed. The ingredients of the story are

REYNE·DE·BATON

III

Queen of Wands   **Three of Pentacles**

Cards from the Minor Arcana showing the four suits (*Also see overleaf*)

presented through powerful symbolism, and it is this which has arguably allowed Tarot to endure through the centuries.

The Soul of the World

The universal significance of these symbols was said by alchemists and mystics to spring from the soul of

Ace of Swords **Knight of Cups**

the world, or *anima mundi*. This was pictured as a kind of vast library, filled with memories and wisdom, which could be consulted through deep contemplation. The great psychiatrist and visionary, Carl Gustav Jung (1875–1961), named this concept the 'collective unconscious'. He wrote, 'The collective unconscious is common to us all; it is the foundation of what the ancients called "the sympathy of all things".'

Within this collective pool dwell archetypal figures which may be found in fairy-tales, myths, legends, religions and Tarot itself. These figures encapsulate a secret storehouse of profound esoteric knowledge: for example, The Empress in Tarot represents the great mother-goddesses of pagan religion, the concept of fertility, and the feminine principle in both psychology and myth. Each figure encourages unconscious knowledge to surface, so that it may be clearly understood and acted upon by the waking, or conscious mind. In a Tarot reading, these figures combine to present a meaningful pattern or story which serves to clarify the enquirer's problems – rather like a memorable dream or sudden vivid flash of inspiration.

Ultimately, Tarot cards are an invaluable tool for both divination and contemplation. By stimulating intuition, they allow the reader and the questioner to understand a situation more clearly and to perceive the hidden elements which may be shaping one's course in life.

HOW TO DO A READING

Tarot is like a language, as knowledge increases so does fluency. Intuition, too, plays a crucial part in any reading, for you are combining the symbols to form a whole, and each card affects the interpretation of the others.

This book gives an interpretation for each of the Major Arcana. Since these are the most complex cards in the whole deck, it is advisable to become familiar with them before trying to do readings using all the cards. Indeed, some experts assert that only the Major Arcana should be used for divination, because they believe this was its original purpose.

Choosing Your Spread

The right layout is a tremendous aid to a good reading. The position of each card refers to a specific area of life, and must be interpreted in that context. Always look at the whole spread first and try to assess the overall feeling of the pattern before you. Are the images especially dramatic ones, such as The Tower? Are they peaceful, like Temperance? Or perhaps the pattern presents a stark series of contrasts. Trust your initial reaction, and then proceed to interpret each individual image.

Two traditional spreads are given here – The Celtic Cross and The Horseshoe. The Celtic Cross is a classic layout, said to be extremely ancient, and is excellent for answering specific questions. Your query must be clearly framed; a confused question can only elicit a puzzling response. The Horseshoe, too, is a reliable spread to use for questions and is simple enough for beginners. Neither spread uses many cards since you will be using the Major Arcana, which not only makes for greater simplicity but often greater accuracy.

Before reading and laying out the cards, they must be shuffled thoroughly by the questioner. During this process, the questioner should concentrate on the matter they wish to find out about. They can either speak their question out loud, or simply think about it in a focused way. Cut the pack three times with the left hand, and re-form it by rearranging the three piles. Deal each card off the top of the deck, and place them in their positions. Some people like to say the name of each position as they lay down the cards, but this is simply a matter of personal preference.

THE CELTIC CROSS
SAMPLE LAYOUT

THE POSITIONS AND THEIR MEANINGS

CARD 1 ☆ *Covering him/her*
Describes the substance of the question, and the enquirer's attitude towards it.

CARD 2 ☆ *Crossing him/her*
Denotes what kind of obstacles must be overcome in the present.

CARD 3 ☆ *Crowning him/her*
Indicates known plans or intentions and immediate developments which might be expected soon.

CARD 4 ☆ *Beneath him/her*
Shows past influences with a direct bearing on the present.

CARD 5 ☆ *Behind him/her*
Denotes influences which are now fading away.

CARD 6 ☆ *Before him/her*
Points to new circumstances coming into being. Cross-reference with Card 3 for a fuller picture.

CARD 7 ☆ *Yourself*
Shows the enquirer's state of mind and feelings about the question. Link this card with Cards 1, 2, 3 and 4 to see how their view has come about.

CARD 8 ☆ *The House*
Indicates what surrounds the enquirer, and the matter at hand.

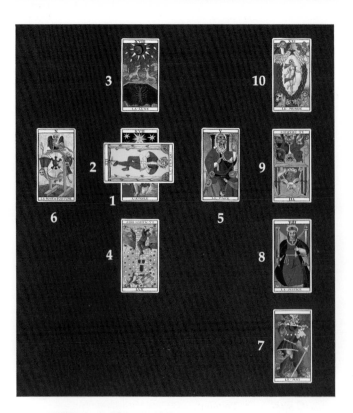

CARD 9 ☆ *Hopes and Fears*
Read in conjunction with Card 3 to see how deep feelings are linked with conscious plans and intentions.

CARD 10 ☆ *What will come*
This card shows the likely future outcome of the circumstances revealed. Remember, a change of attitude towards the problem can alter this result.

THE CELTIC CROSS
INTERPRETATION

The question put to the cards was 'What is my likely career direction in the next six months?' The querist was a self-employed designer, whose career was, necessarily, unstable. He wondered what the future would bring, and thereby sought confirmation that he was, in fact, following the right career path.

CARD 1 ☆ *Covering him*
The Star, in an upright position, indicates that the querist is hopeful and optimistic about his prospects. He could be about to gain fresh inspiration which will encourage him in his endeavours.

CARD 2 ☆ *Crossing him*
The Hanged Man appears as an obstacle to fulfilment and certainty. However, since this card symbolizes rebirth it counsels patience during this apparently stagnant phase.

CARD 3 ☆ *Crowning him*
The Moon augurs unconscious forces at work and reinforces the message of both The Hanged Man and The Star. Renewal is coming, but cannot be hurried.

CARD 4 ☆ *Beneath him*
The Tower reversed reveals that deep-seated feelings of frustration have dogged the querist for some time. He feels trapped in his situation.

CARD 5 ☆ *Behind him*

The Pope suggests that financial worries may have dictated some of his choices, and restricted his creativity as a result.

CARD 6 ☆ *Before him*

The Wheel of Fortune bowls into the spread, heralding unforeseen changes and new contacts. His desire to change is clearly in tune with the times.

CARD 7 ☆ *The Self*

The Fool affirms the message of The Wheel, bringing a breath of fresh air into the querist's life. It also highlights his restlessness, and suggests that some new challenge is badly needed.

CARD 8 ☆ *The Environment*

Justice in this position augurs a decision which is out of his hands, and again links with the message of The Wheel and The Fool. Change is inevitable it would seem.

CARD 9 ☆ *Hopes and Fears*

The Chariot reversed shows that our querist is afraid of losing control of his life and wasting his resources. His lack of confidence may have stopped him branching out in the past.

CARD 10 ☆ *The result*

The World signifies fulfilment and completion. If the querist can overcome feelings of inadequacy and frustration, a new direction and the end of a challenging chapter seem to be in sight.

THE HORSESHOE
SAMPLE LAYOUT

Like the Celtic Cross, each position in this layout represents a precise sphere of influence. By bearing these in mind as you proceed to read the cards you can tailor your interpretation to fit each position. The cards are laid out from right to left.

CARD 1 ☆ *The past*
Denotes past events, actions and feelings pertaining to the question. It is helpful to read this card in conjunction with Card 2, to consider whether much has changed.

CARD 2 ☆ *The present*
Generally indicating what has just occurred, or the enquirer's current state of mind regarding the issue.

CARD 3 ☆ *Hidden influences*
Which are sometimes unexpected, or may represent an alteration in expectations.

CARD 4 ☆ *Obstacles*
Which may be either practical difficulties, or a negative frame of mind.

CARD 5 ☆ *The Environment*
Denotes the attitudes of other people.

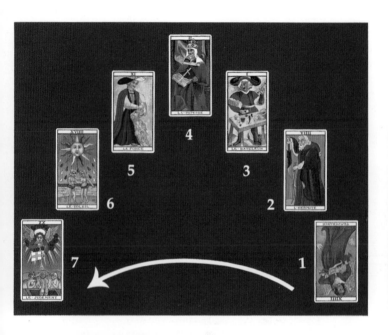

CARD 6 ☆ *What should be done*
This position may offer practical suggestions, or prompt a helpful attitude towards the problem.

CARD 7 ☆ *The most likely result*
Assuming you follow the advice given by Card 6.

THE HORSESHOE
INTERPRETATION

The question asked was 'Will my present relationship develop into something more serious?'

CARD 1 ☆ *The past*
Represented by Temperance. This reveals a balanced attitude towards relationships in general, a willingness to compromise, and a good ability to make friends. This relationship would seem to have a firm foundation.

CARD 2 ☆ *The present*
Represented by The Hermit. This shows that the questioner has adopted a cautious attitude towards involvement. Perhaps they need to spend a little time alone in order to reflect on the future.

CARD 3 ☆ *Hidden influences*
Denoted by The Magician, which is the card of control. This suggests that one or both partners may be holding back in some way. It also points to a need for spontaneity – something unexpected could affect this relationship in the near future.

CARD 4 ☆ _Obstacles_
Denoted by The High Priestess, which signals secrets
and hidden information. This connects to the sponta-
neous event suggested by The Magician. Possibly this
relationship is not quite as it seems on the surface.
One or other party may not be telling the truth about
their feelings, but this will soon be revealed.

CARD 5 ☆ _The Environment_
Strength indicates a positive attitude surrounding the
relationship. This card denotes vitality and courage,
and the power of love. The couple would seem to
have the support of their friends, who have faith in
the relationship.

CARD 6 ☆ _What should be done_
The Sun is the card of pleasure, victory and happiness. Since these do not represent obstacles, this card
reveals that contentment and devotion lie ahead. By
clearing the air, as suggested by both The High
Priestess and The Hermit, the relationship can proceed towards a deeper commitment.

CARD 7 ☆ _Judgement_
Falls in the position of _likely result_. This shows that
the relationship will be reborn, following the period
of readjustment and evaluation indicated by the
previous cards.

PLATE 1
THE FOOL / LE MAT

DIVINATORY MEANING

UPRIGHT Beginnings, most particularly of journeys – mental, physical or spiritual. Surprising solutions. Optimism. Innocence. Spontaneity. Naivety.

REVERSED Ill-advised risks and rash decisions. Gambling. Instability. Foolishness. A bad time to make commitments.

SYMBOLISM

The Fool, brightly dressed in the familiar costume of the court jester, carries all his worldly goods in a knapsack. His companion, a little dog, reminds him of the world of instinct, while his staff represents willpower. He is the eternal child, facing the challenges of life which are symbolized by the remaining twenty-one cards of the Major Arcana.

Fools played a special role in medieval courts, where, protected by their divine madness, they could make fun of everything, and everybody, with impunity. This card recalls a time when irrational behaviour was a sign of possession by a god or spirit, a time when the word 'silly' meant 'blessed'. The figure of the fool is linked with Dionysus, the Greek god of licence and revels; with Parsifal, the naive Arthurian knight; and with the Celtic Green Man, the god of a new life and fertility.

LE · MAT

PLATE 2

I
THE MAGICIAN / LE BATELEUR

DIVINATORY MEANING

UPRIGHT Control over the material world. Self-discipline. Organization. Creative action. Effective communication. Wit. The power to initiate.

REVERSED Confusion. Inability to make a clear-cut choice or decision. Lack of inspiration or energy. Giving up too easily. Negative states of mind.

SYMBOLISM

The Magician or Juggler presides over a table, on which are arranged a number of objects. On closer inspection it is possible to see that these represent three of the suits of the Minor Arcana: the cups, coins, and swords. The suit of Wands is denoted by the wand in his left hand. His hat is shaped in an elipse, reminiscent of the ancient figure-of-eight symbol for eternity. All these symbols remind us that The Magician possesses a wide knowledge of the world, and the ability to manipulate circumstances.

Traditionally, this card is linked with the winged messenger god Hermes / Mercury, who was also god of magic, tricksters, alchemists and language. His wand points upwards to heaven and down to earth, reflecting Hermes' unique ability to travel at will between the heights of Mount Olympus to the depths of the underworld.

PLATE 3

II
THE HIGH PRIESTESS / LA PAPESSE

DIVINATORY MEANING

UPRIGHT Secret knowledge. The importance of intuition. Something remains to be revealed, but you will have to be patient. Mystery. Duality.

REVERSED Repression. Ignorance of true facts or feelings. Hidden enemies. Circumstances are not as they seem.

SYMBOLISM

The High Priestess, or Female Pope, symbolizes feminine spiritual power. In her guise as an actual representative of the Church, she is believed to represent the legendary Pope Joan, who was said to have been elected Pope John VIII in 855. Joan was supposed to have fallen in love with a monk, and dressed as a man in order to be near him. Her lover died but, maintaining her disguise, she became a priest. Her deception was discovered when she disgraced herself by giving birth on the steps of St Peter's in Rome.

Other interpreters link this mysterious card with the goddess Isis in her veiled, or virginal form. Like Isis, the High Priestess holds the book of knowledge and the secrets of regeneration after death. The initiation rituals of the Isis cult were so closely guarded that they remain a tantalizing mystery to this day.

II

LA · PAPESSE

PLATE 4

III
THE EMPRESS / L'IMPÉRATRICE

DIVINATORY MEANING

UPRIGHT Creative fertility in art, parenthood, love and financial affairs. Sensuality. Marriage or commitment. Achievement of goals. Abundance.

REVERSED Financial difficulties. Creative blocks and general lack of achievement. Delay. Problems within a relationship. Lack of affection.

SYMBOLISM

The Empress, crowned and seated upon a throne, is primarily a symbol of feminine power. As such, she is associated with the great fertile mother-goddesses of pagan religion and with the Virgin Mary of Christian tradition. While The High Priestess is veiled and impenetrable, The Empress is both bride and mother. Her earthly power is symbolized here by the eagle on her shield – linking her to The Emperor, her consort. The number of this card is also highly suggestive of its deeper meaning, for three signifies the union of opposites resulting in a new form – whether a child of the body, or the imagination. Three was always associated with the goddess in ancient times because of her triple form, as maiden, mother and crone. She precedes her consort, just as the female-dominated religions of old preceded those ruled by a masculine deity.

III

L'IMPÉRATRICE

PLATE 5

IIII
THE EMPEROR / L'EMPEREUR

DIVINATORY MEANING

UPRIGHT Structure. Worldly power. Competitiveness. Authority. Stability. Ambition coupled with the possibility of long-term achievement.

REVERSED Loss of authority or control. Weakness. Immaturity. Manipulative colleagues or friends. Hatred of authority.

SYMBOLISM

The Emperor is represented as a richly-attired elderly man. His position and power are clearly emphasized by his crown, sceptre, and shield which bears the imperial eagle. As the fourth card of the Major Arcana, The Emperor represents stability, for four is the number of foundation and structure. This meaning is emphasized by his legs, which are positioned like the number four. Traditionally, this is associated with the symbol for sulphur, an active and fiery element. He is linked to all the father-gods of mythology such as Zeus, Jupiter, and Thor. In this role, his energy fertilizes the earth. As consort to The Empress, he represents masculine creativity and parenthood. In pagan terms, he symbolizes the horned god who always partnered the mother goddess.

IIII

L'EMPEREUR

PLATE 6

V
THE POPE / LE PAPE

DIVINATORY MEANING

UPRIGHT Routine and ritual. Marriage. Education in its formal sense. A wise teacher or guide. Sound advice. Partnerships. Morality.

REVERSED Susceptibility. Beware of first impressions. Unconventional behaviour. Rejection of family values. A bad time to sign agreements.

SYMBOLISM

The Pope enjoys the same authority and power as The Emperor, although The Pope's power is spiritual while The Emperor's is temporal. He embodies the true spirit of education in the sense of forming a bridge between this world and the next. His role is to initiate those who seek after knowledge into the sacred mysteries. Accordingly, two supplicants kneel at his feet. His number, five, represents matter (four) united with spirit (one), which suggests his ability to make connections at the highest spiritual levels. He sits before two pillars, which represent good and evil, conscious and unconscious, heaven and hell. He is linked with the powerful Egyptian god of the underworld, Osiris, consort of Isis, who is appropriately associated with The Female Pope or High Priestess.

V

LE · PAPE

PLATE 7

VI
THE LOVERS / L'AMOUREUX

DIVINATORY MEANING

UPRIGHT The beginning of an important romance.
Choices. A struggle between two paths. A test of
some kind. Harmony and union.

REVERSED Infidelity. Disharmony. Deception. A
warning against making important choices at this
time. Romantic disruption.

SYMBOLISM

A young man is shown with two women, one young,
one mature. He is looking to the older woman for
advice, for he seems uncertain about his choice.
Cupid hovers overhead, poised to shoot his arrows of
irrational attraction. Cupid/Eros was the son of the
goddess of love herself, Venus/Aphrodite. He was
often depicted blindfold to symbolize love's blind-
ness. In Tarot, he is said to represent the higher self
which guides us towards the unfolding of our true
destiny. The presence of the older woman is thought
to represent conscious thought and mature decisions.
Many authorities assert that she represents a priestess, poised to advise or marry the young couple. In
ancient times this would have been a natural occurr-
ence, and indeed there were priestesses amongst the
medieval heresies, such as Catharism.

L 'AMOVREVX

PLATE 8

VII
THE CHARIOT / LE CHARIOT

DIVINATORY MEANING

UPRIGHT Well-deserved victory. A period of struggle crowned by worldly success. Effort. Perseverance. Self-discipline.

REVERSED Envy. Avarice. Failure of one's plans. Limitation and loss of self-control. A warning against overweening ambition or expectation.

SYMBOLISM

The Chariot, and its androgynous occupant, are drawn by two horses – one red and one blue. These respectively denote positive and negative, male and female, night and day, past and present. The Charioteer is not driving the vehicle, because he or she has triumphed over conflicting forces and found his or her true path in life. This figure is guided by intuition and acceptance.

As a mythic vehicle, the chariot is found all over the world. In India, the Lord of the World drove his chariot along the road of time, while in ancient Rome, war-like Mars was usually depicted riding triumphantly in his chariot. And the Greek Sun god, Helios, travelled across the skies in his burning chariot of gold. These associations with time and victory express the essence of The Chariot, while its number, seven, is linked with the hidden rhythms of the universe.

VII

LE CHARIOT

PLATE 9

VIII
JUSTICE / LA JUSTICE

DIVINATORY MEANING

UPRIGHT Balance. Justice. Logical decisions. Favourable resolution of conflicts. Clarity. Fairness. A straightforward choice.

REVERSED Imbalance. Delay. Injustice. Complicated negotiations. Confusion regarding tax or legal affairs. Separation.

SYMBOLISM

The figure of Justice remains a familiar one in the modern world. Holding the scales of balance and the sword of truth, her gaze is clear-eyed and impartial. She represents order and integrity, and her mythic lineage stretches all the way back to Ancient Egypt. In Egyptian mythology the goddess Maat, whose name means truth and justice, weighed the souls of the dead against the Feather of Truth – an ancient forerunner of Judgement Day.

This goddess, and versions of her, are also associated with the timeless idea of fate and karma – as you have sown, so shall you reap. This concept informs the Buddhist idea of cause and effect, the Christian belief in sin and redemption, and the Hindu laws of karma. The number eight is also linked with justice and eternity: an old superstition states that there are eight blessings for the virtuous, and eight punishments for the damned.

VIII

LA · JUSTICE

PLATE 10

VIIII
THE HERMIT / L'HERMITE

DIVINATORY MEANING

UPRIGHT Inner calm. Solitude. Prudence. Caution. Discretion. Patience. A wise guide or spiritual mentor. Assimilation.

REVERSED Immaturity. Hastiness. Superficial activity. Foolish obstinacy. Imprudent actions or decisions.

SYMBOLISM

The Hermit represents the archetypal wise old man or sage of myth and legend. He holds his lamp aloft to illuminate the path ahead, and alert others to their true direction. He is supported by a wooden staff which symbolizes the forces of nature and the wisdom of instinct.

The sober appearance of The Hermit is linked to that of Father Time, and the god Saturn/Chronos. He is, therefore, associated with boundaries and limitations. His reclusive nature is a symbolic part of many religions, for initiation rites frequently include a period of silent reflection and withdrawal from the hurly-burly of the material world. The Hermit's number is nine, a number of completion. This signals an important stage on The Fool's journey through the Tarot. It is time to reassess what has been learned prior to a new beginning.

VIIII

L'HERMITE

PLATE 11

X
THE WHEEL OF FORTUNE /
LA ROUE DE FORTUNE

DIVINATORY MEANING

UPRIGHT Coincidences. Luck. The unexpected event that changes one's direction. The appearance of destiny. Positive upheaval and change.

REVERSED Difficulties. Delays. Unexpected interruptions. Bad luck. A warning against gambling.

SYMBOLISM

The Wheel of Fortune is both an ancient symbol in its own right, and a symbol of the Sun's path across the heavens. The creatures attached to the wheel are forever rising and falling according to the dictates of Fate, which is pictured as a monkey-like figure holding a sword.

The message of this picture is one of acceptance of the forces of destiny, and an affirmation of the old adage, 'What goes up must come down'. It encapsulates Eastern philosophical ideas, which invariably speak of balance in all things. Every achievement is followed by a quiet time; every fallow phase precedes an active one. The Wheel of Fortune is a symbolic reminder of the mysterious cycles of death and rebirth, which follow one another like the seasons of the year. Finally, The Wheel denotes wholeness.

X

LA·ROUE·DE·FORTUNE

PLATE 12

XI
STRENGTH / LA FORCE

DIVINATORY MEANING

UPRIGHT The power of love. Courage. Optimism. Energy. Determination. Resolve. Reconciliation. Generosity.

REVERSED Loss of courage. Defeat. Lack of will-power. Pessimism. Inability to act. Tyranny.

SYMBOLISM

A young woman is depicted in the act of opening a lion's mouth. The lion meekly co-operates, suggesting that the woman possesses supernatural powers. Links between women and animals have their roots in the most ancient pagan beliefs in which the Lady of the Animals reigned supreme. She was later personified as the Greek goddess of the hunt, Artemis. The powerful feline goddess of Ancient Egypt, Bastet, and her vengeful sister, the lion-headed Sekhmet, are also linked to this card. Their duality is fused in the card's symbolic meaning, for Bastet stood for fertility and vitality, while Sekhmet denoted violence and death. Strength implies the triumph of love over hatred, and represents the fortitude necessary to overcome even the darkest of challenges.

PLATE 13

XII
THE HANGED MAN / LE PENDU

DIVINATORY MEANING

UPRIGHT Sacrifices. Progress in temporary suspension. A waiting period. Transformation. Rebirth. Circumstances literally upside down.

REVERSED Selfishness and materialism. Loss. Reversal of fortune. Oppression. Failure to act. Inability to move forward.

SYMBOLISM

The Hanged Man is a tantalizing figure, for despite his predicament his expression is serene. Suspended by one foot, he appears to be engaged in some bizarre ritual rather than suffering torture. He is inevitably linked to all the dying and rising gods of mythology, including Atys, the Greek who bled to death beneath a pine tree, and Odin, the Norse god who voluntarily hung from Yggdrasil, the world tree, for nine days and nights. His reward was the magic and knowledge of the runes which he gained following his sacrificial ordeal. Like all the pagan corn gods The Hanged Man symbolically 'dies' in order to be reborn in the spring. Some old Tarot decks name this card 'The Thief' or 'Traitor', linking it with Judas Iscariot who, by betraying Christ, became the unwitting agent of His death and resurrection.

XII

LE · PENDU

PLATE 14

XIII
DEATH / LA MORT

DIVINATORY MEANING

UPRIGHT Transformation. Major changes. Renewal following loss. The end of a phase in life which has fulfilled its purpose.

REVERSED Resistance to change. Inertia. Stagnation. Lethargy. Exhaustion – mental, physical or emotional.

SYMBOLISM

Death, pictured as a skeletal figure wielding a scythe, is portrayed as the Grim Reaper before whom all must fall. For this reason one of the heads is shown with a crown to remind us that all the power and wealth in the world cannot halt the progress of time. In this guise, the image is essentially medieval. Older mythologies often personify death as an all-powerful woman such as the Hindu, Kali, with her necklace of skulls. Death's scythe links the figure with Father Time, symbolizing the inevitability of mortality.

The number thirteen is associated with magic, for it is the number of lunar months in a year, and the traditional number of witches in a coven. In numerology it is both the number of death and destruction, and of hope and rebirth. This, in essence, is the ultimate message of the card which, although macabre, promises that new life follows disintegration.

PLATE 15

XIIII
TEMPERANCE / TEMPÉRANCE

DIVINATORY MEANING

UPRIGHT Literally, temperance in the sense of balance and harmony. Combination. Co-operation. Successful negotiations. Diplomacy.

REVERSED Imbalance. Disagreements. Poor judgement. Instability and restlessness. Physical stress.

SYMBOLISM

An angel pours water between two vessels, symbolizing the eternal flow of the waters of life. Both vessels, water and the angel herself represent the feminine principles of receptivity, harmony, and creativity. They also denote the flow of time; in some old decks Temperance was named 'Time'. The name of this card contains the key to its symbolic meaning, for *temperare* in Latin means to moderate, blend, or mix harmoniously.

Numbered fourteen, Temperance is also linked with the Moon's cycles, for on the fourteenth day the Moon is at the exact midway point of its monthly journey. The ancient Assyrians held special ritual ceremonies on this day in honour of their goddess.

XIIII

TEMPÉRANCE

PLATE 16

XV
THE DEVIL / LE DIABLE

DIVINATORY MEANING

UPRIGHT The material world. Money matters. Security versus spiritual or creative fulfilment. Sexual obsession. Lust.

REVERSED The abuse of power. Greed. Ego. Bondage to a situation or person. Emotional blackmail. Exhaustion.

SYMBOLISM

The Devil is, superficially, one of the more alarming cards in the Major Arcana. However, this card does not herald satanic forces, and it is important to realize this when interpreting it. Fundamentally, The Devil is simply the old horned god of pagan fertility rites who was banished by the established Church. The card's links with lust and sexuality bear witness to its links with Pan, the universal deity of Greek mythology, and also Dionysus, whose wild mythic followers, the satyrs, also had goats' legs.

The two chained figures on the card relate to material bondage, that is, an over-emphatic attachment to money and status objects. Their chains are loose, symbolizing their potential for freedom whenever they choose to turn their backs on obsession.

XV

LE · DIABLE

PLATE 17

XVI
THE TOWER / LA MAISON DIEU

DIVINATORY MEANING

UPRIGHT Major changes. Disruption of settled routines. Anger. Dramatic upheaval. Ultimately, freedom and enlightenment.

REVERSED Sudden changes out of one's control. Imprisonment and restriction of desires. Negativity. Oppression.

SYMBOLISM

A tall tower is being struck by a great fiery bolt of lightning. Two figures tumble to the earth below. This is a dramatic card, traditionally linked with the Biblical story of the Tower of Babel. This impressive edifice was intended by its builders to reach up to heaven. The builders longed to make war on God and his angels, for they sought to avenge their ancestors who were drowned when God caused the rains that flooded the world. But He made them speak in different tongues, so that they were unable to communicate with each other, and their tower never fulfilled its purpose.

The lightning on the card is linked both with the Christian God, especially of the Old Testament, and with the Greek god, Zeus – ruler of all the gods and goddesses on Mount Olympus. It strikes suddenly, denoting the 'out of the blue' quality associated with this card.

PLATE 18

XVII
THE STAR / L'ÉTOILE

DIVINATORY MEANING

UPRIGHT Renewal of faith and hope. Healing old wounds. Joy in nature. Spiritual love. Protection. Inspiration.

REVERSED Pessimism. Tension. Stubbornness. Lack of trust. Self-doubt. Inability to express oneself freely.

SYMBOLISM

A naked woman pours the contents of two vessels into a pool, and on to the land beside her. She is naked because she represents unveiled truth and the purity of hope. The waters of life, which are also depicted on Temperance, are here being poured out to infuse the land with new life. Above this figure seven stars illuminate the night sky, surrounding a larger one shining more brightly than the rest. The presence of these stars suggests links with a number of ancient religions including Greek, Red Indian, Egyptian and Sumerian. The large central star symbolizes the goddess of love and hope, surrounded by her handmaidens. *Stella Maris* ('Star of the Sea') was one of the titles of Aphrodite/Venus and is said to refer to the planet itself which may be seen, sparkling alone, as the morning and evening star. In old numerological systems this card's number, seventeen, was linked with immortality, self-expression, intuition and hope.

XVII

L'ÉTOILE

PLATE 19

XVIII
THE MOON / LA LUNE

DIVINATORY MEANING

UPRIGHT Dreams, imagination and psychic impressions. The unconscious mind. Illusions. Losing control of one's daily life.

REVERSED Trickery. Insincere people. Dangerous
fantasies. Hidden forces. The need for secrecy.

SYMBOLISM

The Moon is depicted in all its phases, riding high in
the night sky. Two towers denote the gateways to the
unconscious, a message which is reiterated by the
pool containing a crayfish-like creature. The pool is
said by many interpreters to denote our earliest
stages of development. As we crawl out of it, we
develop awareness and aspire to a deeper and fuller
understanding of life and its meaning.

Beside the pool, two dogs howl in unison. The
combination of dogs and moon has links with numer-
ous mythologies, most of them focused upon the
central idea of a death deity. Anubis, jackal-headed
god of the Egyptian underworld; Pluto and his
guardian hound, triple-headed Cerebus; and Hecate,
goddess of midwives, witchcraft and queen of the
underworld, are three examples of such a deity. Dogs
are said to be sensitive to the approach of the Angel
of Death, a superstitious reminder of these ancient
beliefs.

XVIII

LA·LUNE

PLATE 20

XVIIII
THE SUN / LE SOLEIL

DIVINATORY MEANING

UPRIGHT Vitality, mental, physical and spiritual. Happiness and joy. Confidence. Success. Children. Achievement.

REVERSED Doubt and uncertainty. Failure of plans. Vanity. Arrogance. Happiness delayed. Relationship difficulties.

SYMBOLISM

The Sun blazes brightly in a golden sky, while two little children play on the earth beneath. These children symbolize the fruit of the previous card, The Moon, which, with its deep connections to what is hidden, represents gestation. The Sun symbolizes birth – or, in psychological terms, the union between the unconscious and conscious minds which precedes true creativity.

The enduring symbol of the Sun itself is recognizable all over the world as a representation of hope, light, life and warmth. The ancient Egyptians, led by the pharaoh, Akhenaton, worshipped the Sun as the living god, Aton, bringer of beauty, love and fertility to the earth. To the Greeks, he was Apollo, god of prophecy, healing, music and the arts. His mythic energy and vitality remain the symbolic essence of this uplifting Tarot image.

XVIIII

LE · SOLEIL

PLATE 21

XX
JUDGEMENT / LE JUGEMENT

DIVINATORY MEANING

UPRIGHT Decision-making. Renewed mental clarity. Rebirth. Changes and improvements. A good time to make career moves.

REVERSED Delayed decisions. Stagnation. Fear of change. Loss and separation, not necessarily permanent.

SYMBOLISM

One of the most purely Christian images of the Major Arcana, Judgement depicts Judgement Day when the souls of the dead are called to rise up from their graves. Archangel Michael blows his horn, summoning everyone to the moment of final reckoning.

This idea of resurrection does, of course, predate Christian myth and dogma; while the concept of judgement is also linked with the prevailing eastern belief in reincarnation and karma. The message of all these doctrines is the same: your deeds and decisions in life are never without consequence, even after you are dead. Judgement is the penultimate card of the Major Arcana, symbolizing rebirth and initiation prior to completion of one's spiritual journey.

PLATE 22

XXI
THE WORLD / LE MONDE

DIVINATORY MEANING

UPRIGHT The completion of a cycle or chapter in life. Success. Accomplishment. Fulfilment.

REVERSED Completion delayed. Frustration. Resistance to change or growth. Lack of trust. Hesitation.

SYMBOLISM

A naked woman dances inside an oval wreath. Each corner contains a symbolic creature: an angel, an eagle, a bull and a lion. These creatures are linked to the four 'fixed' signs of the Zodiac – Aquarius, Scorpio, Taurus and Leo, and with the four elements – fire, earth, air and water. Together they symbolize the balance and completion which is this card's essential message.

The female figure on the card has often been thought to represent an hermaphrodite, denoting the perfect blending of masculine and feminine attributes which is the ultimate aim of mysticism, alchemy and some schools of psychoanalysis. Other scholars maintain that the figure is that of the great mother-goddess herself, who in ancient myths created the earth and everything in it. Both schools of thought agree that the joyful dance denotes the eternal dance of life, death, and rebirth.

XXI

LE · MONDE

PICTURE ACKNOWLEDGEMENTS

Frontispiece The Magician from the Pierpont-Morgan Visconti-Sforza Tarocchi deck reproduced by permission of U.S. Games Systems, Inc., Stamford, CT 06902 USA. Copyright © 1975, 1984 by U.S. Games Systems, Inc. Further reproduction prohibited.

All other cards used in this book are from the Tarot of Marseille pack produced by Heraclio Fournier, S.A., Spain. This pack is generally available from major high street bookshops and specialist occult bookshops.